Old Tales, New Pages

A Tale
of
A Tail

A Simple Curve,
A Difficult Task

Laxmi Balaji

◆◆◆◆◆◆◆◆◆◆◆◆◆◆◆◆◆◆
To the two little readers who call me
'Mom' and the man who helps me find
the words. Because of you, I always have
a story to tell.
◆◆◆◆◆◆◆◆◆◆◆◆◆◆◆◆

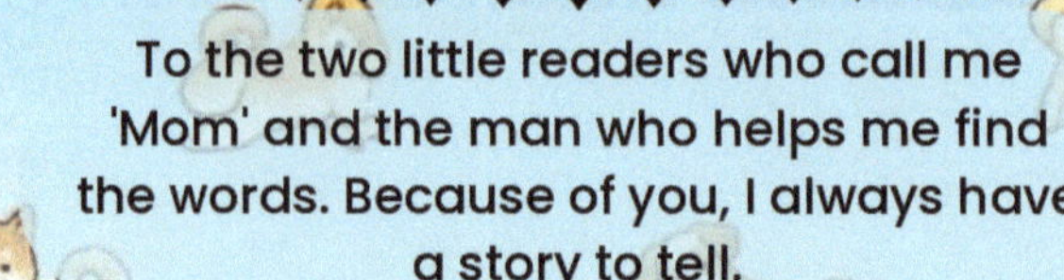

Old Tales, New Pages

A Tale of a Tail
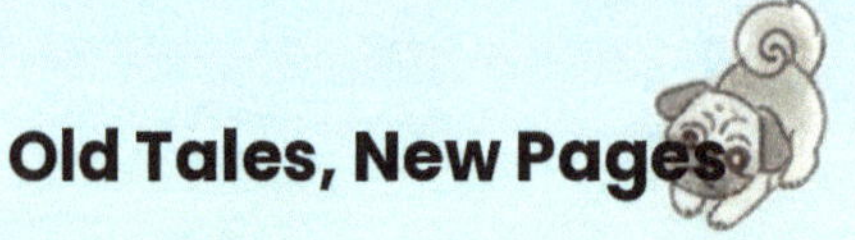
(A Simple Curve, A Difficult Task)

For every clever Disciple who knows that the simplest answer is
often the best. A hilarious tale about what happens when brute
force meets the most stubborn curl in all of nature

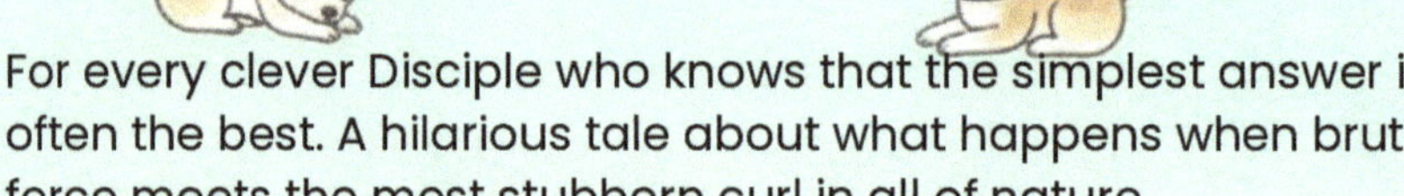

Sagas-R-Us
Laxmi Balaji
www.sagasrus.ca

ISBN (Paper back): 978-1-0698740-4-7
ISBN (E-Book): 978-1-0698740-5-4

There once was a powerful magician, a Manthiravati, who was always trying to be more powerful. One day he decided that his magic just wasn't enough!

"I shall do ferocious tapas!" he declared. "I will get so much power, I will control the whole world! You watch the ashram, Disciple."

The Disciple, who was very clever and very calm, just sighed. "What else is new?" he muttered, knowing his master always got into trouble.

So the Manthiravati walked deep into the forest, where the ancient trees stood shoulder-to-shoulder and sunlight dared not reach. There, far from the sounds of the ashram, he began his tapas: a fierce, unyielding session of prayer and meditation, determined to force the Gods to grant him his wish.

God eventually showed up.

"What do you want this time?" asked God.

"I want the whole world! In the palm of my hand!" demanded the Manthiravati, showing his palm.

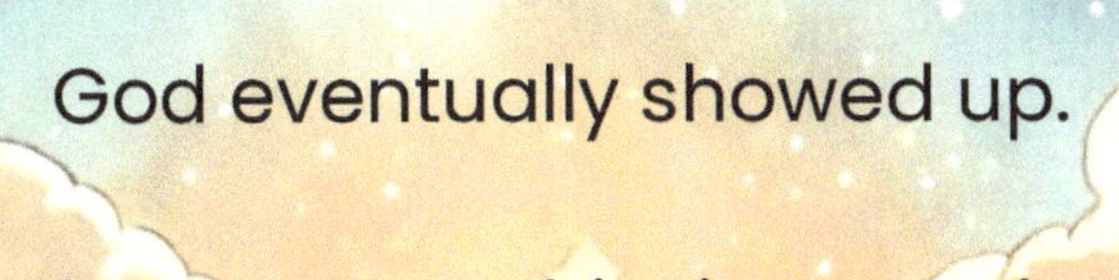

"Hmm," said God. "The world's bigger than your palm, you know."

"I don't care! I want that kind of power!"

God gave in. He called the leader of the demons, the Bhuta.

"Bhuta," God instructed, "you must now obey this Manthiravati. Do whatever he says. Don't refuse anything."

The Bhuta, who was HUGE and built like a mountain, looked disappointed. "Fine," he grumbled and rolled his eyes. "But I have one rule. I must be kept busy every single day. If I ever run out of work, I will get hungry. And when I get hungry.... I eat him!"

"Work, Work, Give me more!
Stomp the ground and Hear me roar!
Make it fast, Make it grand!
Magic comes from this Bhuta's hand!"
Said the Bhuta!

The Manthiravati gulped and said. "That's fine! I have loads of work! You can't possibly finish it!"

On the way to the ashram, the Manthiravati was thinking and realized his mistake.

As soon as they reached the ashram, they went to his disciple. "Disciple! I made a big mistake!" shrieked the Manthiravati. "I got this Bhuta, and if he runs out of work, he eats us up! You give him the jobs. You're the smart one!"

And with that, the terrified Manthiravati ran away and hid!

The next morning, the Bhuta showed up, stomping his foot.

"Work, Work, Give me more!
Stomp the ground and Hear me roar!
Make it fast, Make it grand!
Magic comes from this Bhuta's hand!"
Said the Bhuta.

The Disciple had an idea. "All right! See those empty lands? Cut down every tree, level the ground, and build us TWO GOLDEN MANSIONS—made entirely of jewels—before sundown!"

The Bhuta roared with laughter. He blew hard, and all the trees flew miles away. He whistled, and thousands of little Bhutas appeared! In just TWO HOURS, they built two glittering mansions of rubies, diamonds, and emeralds!

The Bhuta came back, folded his massive arms, and scowled. "Look at the mansions! They sparkle!"

"Work, Work, Give me more!
Stomp the ground and Hear me roar!
Make it fast, Make it grand!
Magic comes from this Bhuta's hand!"
Said the Bhuta.

"GIVE ME MORE WORK Tomorrow!"

The next day, the Bhuta was back. "That was nothing! Give me some real work!"

"Work, Work, Give me more!
Stomp the ground and Hear me roar!
Make it fast, Make it grand!
Magic comes from this Bhuta's hand!"
Said the Bhuta.

The clever Disciple pointed to the giant ocean. "Look at that ocean. You must empty it completely before nightfall. Not one drop remains!"

The Bhuta scoffed. Pft, an ocean? Too easy!

SCLURP!
GULP!
GULP!
GULP!
SLURP! The Bhuta took one huge swallow, and half the ocean was gone! GULP! He took a second huge swallow, and the entire ocean was just a dry, sandy bed!
It was only evening! The Bhuta came back, tapping his foot. "Done! The ocean is gone! GIVE ME MORE WORK Tomorrow!"
The Disciple started to worry. "He's fast! He is too fast! This Bhuta is a big trouble!"

The next day Bhuta came again asking for more work.
"Work, Work, Give me more!
Stomp the ground and Hear me roar!
Make it fast, Make it grand!
Magic comes from this Bhuta's hand!"
Said the Bhuta.

The Disciple already thought hard and came well prepared for Bhuta. He said, "Take every grain of sand on the beach and separate it into three piles: fine sand, medium sand, and coarse sand." The Disciple thought it will take forever for him to finish his work.

"Thats easy" said Bhuta, He claps his hands, creating a magical vortex. The piles of different sands appear instantly. "Blink, blink! Blink! Done!!"

The next day, Bhuta asked for more work.

"Work, Work, Give me more!
Stomp the ground and Hear me roar!
Make it fast, Make it grand!
Magic comes from this Bhuta's hand!"
Said the Bhuta.

The Disciple said, "Take the entire chain of the Himalayas, smooth out every peak, and turn them into a perfectly leveled for farming!"

The Bhuta takes one giant leap towards the mountains. There was a tremendous sound BADOOM! Then, he uses his massive hands to smash and smooth the peaks down like mud pies, instantly transforming the sharp mountains into a perfectly level field.

BADOOM!

That night, the Disciple paced in his new golden mansion. "I have to get rid of him. He is too fast! I need something impossible, but harmless!"

Just then, a dog waddled past and paused outside the gate. The Disciple looked at its tail, which was curled into a perfect, tight roll.

Ah-ha! he came up with an idea.

The next morning, the Bhuta came stomping. "What's up for today?"

"Work, Work, Give me more!
Stomp the ground and Hear me roar!
Make it fast, Make it grand!
Magic comes from this Bhuta's hand!"
Said the Bhuta.

The Disciple smiled calmly. "Listen. See that dog? Your job today is to straighten its tail. It must be PERFECTLY STRAIGHT before dark. You cannot hurt the dog, you can't cut its hair, and you can't leave a single scratch. It must just be straight!"

The Bhuta just laughed. "A dog's tail? That's not a job, that's a nap!"

The Bhuta gave the dog the biggest steak, it had ever seen. He waited until the dog fell into a deep, meaty sleep.

The Bhuta gently grabbed the tail, smoothed the hair, and stretched it out straight. "Perfect!" he whispered. He let it go.

"Boing went the tail and woof said the dog!" The tail coiled right back up!

The Bhuta tried again. He pulled the tail, massaged it, he whispered sweet things to it. He let it go.

"Boing went the tail and woof said the dog!" It curled right back up!

He tried to smear the tail with butter! And he let it go.

"Boing went the tail and woof said the dog!" Still curled!

Finally, the Bhuta found a stick and some silk thread. He carefully splinted the tail, tying it tightly to the stick. He waited some time. Then, he untied it.

"Boing went the tail and woof said the dog!" Back into a tight roll!

He tried and tried, but that stubborn tail just kept SNAPPING BACK!

The Bhuta got frustrated.

The sun went down. The Bhuta looked at the curled tail, looked at his massive hands, and realized he had failed the simple task.

He was defeated by a single, tiny, furry curl! He hung his giant head in shame and vanished forever.

The Manthiravati crept out of hiding the next day. "Is he gone? Did he not eat you?"

The Disciple just pointed to the two glittering mansions.

"What did you do?" asked the Manthiravati.

"I remembered the old saying: **'The one thing you can't make straight in this world is a dog's tail!'** that's all" said the disciple.

And the two of them lived a rich and very peaceful life in their golden homes, forever grateful to the curliest, and unstraightenable dog's tail in the world.

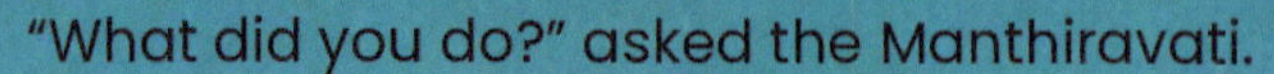

Glossary

Manthiravati (mun-thi-rah-VAAH-thee) - Sorcerer. A person who performs magic, spells, or enchantments for personal gain.

Tapas(TAH-pus) - Intense Effort. Performing difficult tasks (like fasting or deep meditation) to gain spiritual power or a gift from a god.

Disciple (dih-SY-pill) - Student. A person who learns from and follows a master.

Bhuta (BOO-tah) - A powerful being, often a large or supernatural entity (in this story, a powerful demon).

Ashram (Aa -sh-rum) - Hermitage. A religious retreat, school, or community where a teacher and their disciples live.

Swami (SWAH-mee) - Master. A respectful title used for a revered teacher, spiritual leader, or monk.

Did you know that the idea of trying to straighten a dog's tail is a very old proverb? It's often used to mean that you can't change a person's habits or nature, no matter how hard you try. The Bhuta learned that you really can't fight nature!

It wasn't just magic that kept the tail curled! For many dogs, their naturally curly tails are that way because the bones in their tail—the vertebrae—are wedge-shaped on one side. That means the tail is designed to curve, and no amount of pulling, butter, or splints can change the shape of those little bones! Pity Bhuta did not know this!

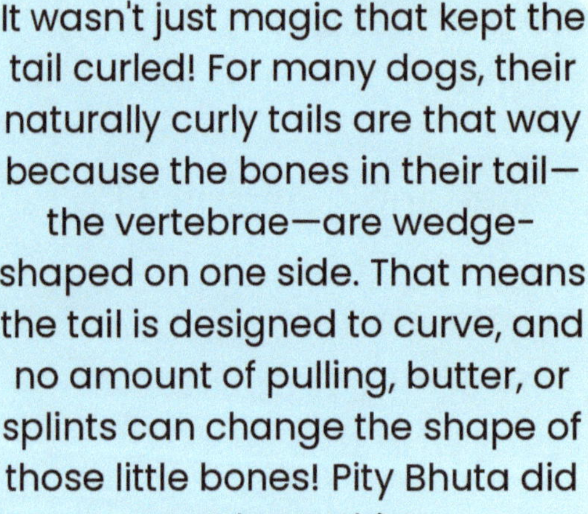

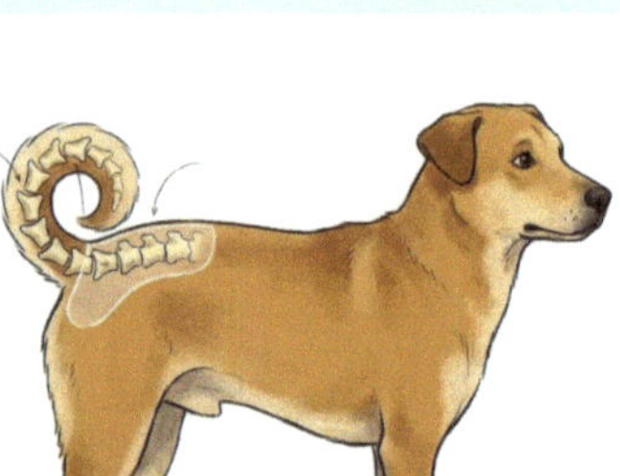

Even when curled up, a dog's tail is vital! It helps them with balance when running and turning, and it's their main way of showing us how they feel. That Bhuta should have just focused on getting a happy wag instead of a straight line!

Scientists have actually studied tail wags! When a dog wags its tail more to the right side, it often means they are happy and relaxed. But if it wags more to the left? That might mean they are nervous or unsure. The Bhuta was probably causing a lot of left-side wagging!

For fast dogs, the tail is a built-in counterbalance! When a dog runs really fast and needs to make a super-sharp turn, it whips its tail the other way to stop itself from falling over. It's like a built-in steering wheel—a furry, powerful rudder!

Did you know tail-wagging is a learned skill? Puppies don't start wagging their tails to say hello until they are about four to six weeks old. Once they start talking to their mother and siblings, they start learning this skill. The Bhuta was working on a truly ancient skill!